Portfolio of
Painterly Poems

Portfolio of Painterly Poems

A Pilgrim's Path to God

Sharon R. Chace

Resource Publications
An imprint of Wipf and Stock Publishers
Eugene, Oregon

Resource Publications
An imprint of Wipf and Stock Publishers
199 West 8th Avenue, Suite 3
Eugene, OR 97401

Portfolio of Painterly Poems: A Pilgrim's Path to God
Copyright©2006 by Sharon R. Chace
ISBN: 1-59752-632-0
Publication Date: April 2006

*Dedicated in memory and celebration of Pat Hale,
who was first to notice buds on winter trees.*

Thank you to my husband Ernest, who supports me with enthusiasm and hours of photocopying. Daughter Amy continually gives the gift of faith in Mom. Sharon Martin Kachmar read my manuscript and encouraged me to find a publisher who would include my art. I thank her for her suggestions that have helped me polish my work and her happiness in seeing me shine poetically.

Without frequent publication in the Meriden, Connecticut RECORD-JOURNAL poetry column, *Pennons of Pegasus*, edited by Lois Lake Church, I would not have written enough poems for a book. Thank you to Lois for nurturing poets. I am deeply appreciative of the work of typesetter, Kimberly Medgyesy.

Table of Contents

Introduction   xv

Calling

HAIKU HEARKENING	3
EBB TIDE	4
HIGH TEA JAM	6
OTHER TASKS	7
KINDRED SPIRIT DOG	8
AFFINITY	9
LANGUAGE	10
EMERGENCE	11
PLANT POWER	12
POET'S REVIEW: *Letters on Cézanne* Rainer Maria Rilke	14
JUST WHEN	15

MOXIE	16
POET'S PLAN	17
JOURNEY TO THE SUN	18

Continuance

ART CLASS SONNET	21
ART PAD NOTES	22
SOPHOMORE SONNET Albion College, 1963	24
LOVE SONG	25
OLD MAN	26
SUMMER	27
PROMISE	28
DRAINED	29
CHURCH MOUSE	30
GOOD DAY	32
THE FIRE	34
DEACONESS	36
CHURCH TALK	38
LOVE SONNET	39
MOMENTS	40
LIGHT HAPPENS IN HAIKU	42
PERMANENCE	43
SHADES	44
FRAGMENT	45

ECLIPSE AND LIGHT	46
REVELATION	48
TWO TRIPS	50
AGING	52
PRIORITY	53
SHOPPING LIST	54
CORNFLOWER HAIKU	56
THE OTHER CHURCH	57
MEANWHILE	58
MOVE TO MERIDEN	59
STYLES	60
HAIKU SEASONING	62
NEW ENGLAND FALL	68
SILENT WAITING	70
WINTER STORM	71
WINTER RETREAT	72
NEW HAMPSHIRE GLORY	73
APRIL BLESSING	74
GIFTS OF TIME AND MINDS	75
CELEBRATION IS…	76
CLOUDY BEACH DAY	77
BLACK ROCKS	78
OTHER COLORS, OTHER ROCKS	79
DAY OF THE STARFISH	80

MAINE HAIKU	83
CONNECTICUT DAYS	84
DAD	85
TO SAPPHO	86
BROWN AND WHITE DOG IN OILS	87
STANCE OF CHOICE	88
SKY MEMORIES	90
DAWN	92
CONFESSIONS	93
YOU KNOW	94
RE: 9/11	95
REFRESH	96
GARDEN VARIETY	97
A GRACE	98
CITRUS SIMMERING	99
AUBADE	100
FALL SONNET	101
MOMENTUM SONNET	102

Completion

PARADOX	105
HAIKU HOMING	106
TRIP HOME	108
GREEN SCENE	109

HAIKU WREATH	110
ON ROUTE (To Westmoreland, NH)	112
SONNET FOR DORIS	113
ETERNAL AUBADE	114
WIDENING STREAM	116
IMAGINING	118
GETTING THERE	121
THE MIND OF GOD	122
ONE PURE NOTE	124
TRANSLATION	127
BLUE SONNET	128
POSTSCRIPT	129
Acknowledgments	131

Introduction

I am an artist and poet. In a way, I was a poet and artist even before I could print my name or color inside the lines, although thinking inside the lines has never been my style. My first awareness of the beauty of color came at age three through cobalt blue vases on the windowsill. In a twinkling of light, blue became my first favorite color and link to my terminally-ill mother, a former librarian and fine painter in oils, who colored with me. Painterly companionship mattered and became good memories. Blue, which evokes promise of transcendent meaning, gave aesthetic nourishment that would last a lifetime. Other colors would grow in importance. The first haiku in HAIKU WREATH suggests the flow of my life. Small white butterfly / flits from sad blue violets / to bright bold tulips.

    Beauty mattered. The importance of truth dawned in my impressionable mind. Following the conventional wisdom of the time, my father did not want anyone talking with me about death. The only person who did was the minister who visited the playgroup I attended at the Universalist Church in Gloucester, Massachusetts. Although I do not remember the exact conversation, I do remember building with blocks as we talked. Unlike beauty and truth, which partake of the eternal, my play structures toppled. When truth and beauty are important, poetry may follow.

Portfolio of Painterly Poems

Overhearing conversations about religion called forth my curiosity. My grandmother, called Bessie by everyone, and her friend Katie often took care of me. Grandmother Bessie was an agnostic. Katie was a Protestant evangelical. They constantly talked about religion. In retrospect, I wanted to be in on the discussion of what it means to be religious. Interest in religion complemented my painterly art. In a personal fullness of time, theological aesthetics became the focal point of my life.

Before I could write, I composed poems and prayers in pretend writing, stick lines on paper, and placed them with my dolls' tea parties on the top of my bureau, symbolically nearer God. Nature pushed. Grace pulled. Art classes, Girl Scout activities and working in the public library were joys woven throughout my school days in my hometown, Rockport, Massachusetts. It was a great privilege to have artist Joseph Jeswald, a founder of the Montserrat School of Art in Beverly Massachusetts, for my high school art teacher. The Pilgrim Fellowship of the First Congregational Church gave strength for living through prayer, play and purpose.

College offered expanding vistas. I majored in art and had minors in English and religion at Albion College in Albion, Michigan, graduating in 1966 with a B.A. Over thirty years later in 1998, I received a Master of Theological Studies (M.T.S.) from Weston Jesuit School of Theology in Cambridge, Massachusetts, where I was a middle-aged Protestant wildcard. My concentration was biblical studies. I participated in poetry readings and had a one-person art show of watercolor and collage paintings in the combined libraries of Weston Jesuit School of Theology and Episcopal Divinity School. I have also studied at Andover Newton Theological School and Harvard and Yale Divinity Schools. My poems, essays and short stories have been published in a variety of journals.

My husband Ernest was a United Church of Christ minister for ten years. We served parishes in Walpole, New Hampshire, and Verona, New Jersey. Sermons written on graph paper were a sign that Ernest is really an engineer at heart. His most peaceful

Introduction

moments came as gift when looking through the lens of his camera. Likewise, I was blessed with the opportunity to study watercolor painting with Nora S. Unwin at the Sharon Arts Center in Peterborough, New Hampshire.

Parish life provided some of the poetic ingredients that stew in my crock-pot mind. I am a really slow cooker. Pondering is an asset, I believe, in a creative life of discovering the best word or discerning the painterly nuances between crimson and rose madder. My most genuine calling or way of giving back to life and God is sharing art of paint and pen. Our daughter Amy Elizabeth, who played with the toy camera in the nursery of the Walpole church, is a photographer, illustrator and poet. Creative processes continue.

CALLING

Calling

HAIKU HEARKENING

Peony beckons.
Little child smelling sweetness
falls into blossoms.

My life is about
distillation and essence.
Haiku is apt form.

Portfolio of Painterly Poems

EBB TIDE

Ebb Tide, the received title of
my high school newspaper,
in retrospect reflects a
colossal, collective, low
self-esteem, because we
were clueless, unaware of
abilities to contribute beyond
small town community.
Or maybe *Ebb Tide* hides
a barely conscious, communal
celebration of low tide treasures:
lively crabs in tide pools, purplish
blue mussel shells with pearled
white insides, beer-bottle brown
beach glass and sea glass in
shades of green and aquamarine.
Cobalt blue is now a prized
surprise because Noxzema
now comes in plastic.

Calling

I harbor a notion that somewhere
an artist will toss deep-blue
glass into the ocean for new
generations to find, then with
spirits flowing from beauty
to high tide, mine their insistent,
interior treasures.

Portfolio of Painterly Poems

HIGH TEA JAM

The confines of my life
serve to conserve strength.
Seeds sown in silent stillness
swell, then burst their hulls
and blossom into mind fruit.
Cherries of the soul simmer,
boil down into sweet preserve,
a foretaste, a bow to the
Eternal Now.

Calling

OTHER TASKS

Knit five. Purl five.
Contradictory stitches
match the tension in my
tangled knots in thought.
Having made baby blankets
the church fair cannot sell
and Church World Service
does not want,
knitting is penance except
for the grace of
knit five, purl five.
Curled, narrow strips flow
through my fingers like
ribbons in a Morris Louis
abstract contemplation.
Braiding and coiling
solid and variegated,
pale and saturated hues
into rugs - I think of
of other things to do.

Portfolio of Painterly Poems

KINDRED SPIRIT DOG

Everyday, Friga, a dog of mixed-breed body and collie face, stopped by our house on the north of Boston coast for her daily, doggie biscuit. On the day before she died, she looked at me for a long time as if to say goodbye and to remember everything about my face and each detail of our home, like poets do, even those with many future, sacred moments to behold and hold.

Calling

AFFINITY

I tried to find
significance in
attraction:
a dragonfly
lighting on my knee.
Maybe insects just
like me.
Affinity is enough.

Portfolio of Painterly Poems

LANGUAGE

Ambitious verbs,
Strong nouns
In concrete,
Abstract nouns
Distilling elemental
Matter and motifs,
Astonishing adjectives,
Gowned in fancy,
Flowering adverbs
All play a part in the
Diagram of grammar.
Sometimes there is
Pleasure to be found
Even in strung nonsense
Words with soothing
Alliteration from sounds.

Calling

EMERGENCE

Red-green,
Thesis-antithesis,
The dynamics of
Complementary colors
Drive the inner
Momentum of art
Towards harmony
As thesis-antithesis
Propels the development
Of thought to synthesis.
Hence complementary
Colors are to the artist
What a dialectic thought
Process is to a philosopher.
I remember the first time,
Around sixth grade, that
I found the energy of red and
Green in a sumac branch.
Thinking dialectically would
Wait until a later date, as if
By fate, colors and ideas,
Art and philosophy, melded
As complements in the
Synthesis of poetry.

Portfolio of Painterly Poems

PLANT POWER

I hold to the promise
of the tansy, a sign
divine to see.
Seeded, designed-desires
decree decisively.
Rooted heart-hopes
bloom as courage to
be–then spiral freely,
blithely, encouragingly.
In a book of 1896, *The
Country of the Pointed Firs*,
by Sarah Orne Jewett,
bright, yellow clusters of
button flowers, like little
happy suns, symbolize
strength for work to be done.
The tansy that grew around
the schoolhouse had snap.
" Being scuffed down all
the spring made it grow so
much the better, like some
folks that had it hard in their
youth, and were bound to
make the most of themselves
before they died."

Calling

Snap, snap. Craft calls me.
I hold to the promise of
the tansy.

Portfolio of Painterly Poems

POET'S REVIEW
Letters on Cézanne
Rainer Maria Rilke

Eighty years before PhotoShop,
a poet saw brightness/contrast
and saturation/hue in Cézanne's
 blues: "thunderstorm blue: bourgeois,
cotton blue; densely quilted blue;
 juicy blue; waxy and wet dark blue."

At the start of modern art and the
imploding of the modern era when
the center could not hold, a poet
viewed the interconnection of colors
"as if every part were aware of the
others…" and discerned "how
each daub plays its part in maintaining
equilibrium."

In his time, extending into ours and
onto timelessness, a poet perceived that
Cézanne "knew how to swallow back
his love for every apple and put it to
rest in the painted apple for ever."
Resolve to art's best – Regards to you,
Mr. Rilke.

Calling

JUST WHEN

Just when I think
a poem is finished,
it is not.
Just when I feel that
there is not one more
poem in me, there is.
Just when I wonder if
it would be fun to go
back it time with Beowulf
and cookie-swaps ahead,
I say NO WAY.
The past can stay.
For poets, agile aging
and renewed naivete
playfully convey dawning,
dancing May days
of urgency and spring.

Portfolio of Painterly Poems

MOXIE

My grandmother, Bessie,
as everyone called her,
drank MOXIE® and gave
me some in a child-sized glass.
The general consensus was
that she had a lot of moxie,
metaphor for grit and gumption.
I've read in *The New York Times*
about new energy drinks.
Yet, *as it may be*,* I'll find
my measured beat in moxie.

                      *AS IT MAY BE: A Story of the Future
                                Bessie Story Rogers, 1905.

Calling

POET'S PLAN

Some day I will have a book,
**PORTFOLIO
OF PAINTERLY POEMS**
There will be three parts.
Calling
Continuance
Completion
Rest can wait.
I hope the longest section is
Continuance.

Portfolio of Painterly Poems

JOURNEY TO THE SUN

When stars seem
out of reach, it is time
to consider feet.
Claim the symbol of
keeping on trudging and
meter-measure of
striving and trying.
Revisit the Puritan past.
Join the Pilgrim on
his progress and trust
in "shoes and prayers."

CONTINUANCE

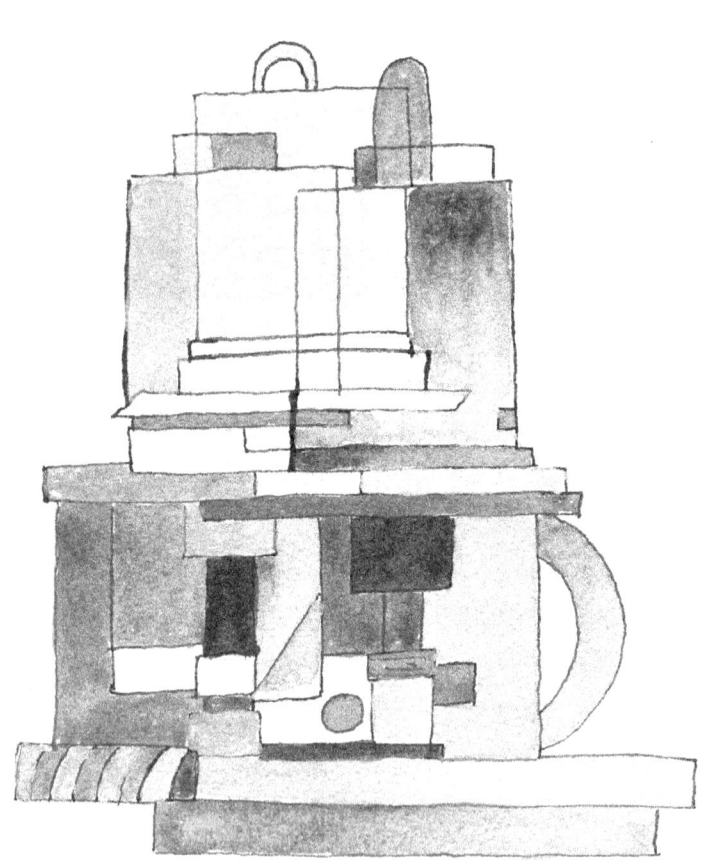

Continuance

ART CLASS SONNET

Art class the warm summer when I turned nine,
By lovely Evelyn Longley taught.
I rode the bus from Pigeon Cove each time
Favorite days when colors all I sought.
Sunshine, white clouds and Motif # One
Rockport icon drawn, painted carefully.
My word-free, arty world had just begun
Line, love, texture ahead applied fully.
Mixed blue and white made perfect, summer sky
To remember on future, foggy days.
In time, too soon, we had to say *Goodbye*.
Color memories keep sadness at bay.
There is present sense of eternal time.
Art goes on—creative process assigned.

Portfolio of Painterly Poems

ART PAD NOTES

Most of the time,
the stripe down the
middle of daylily leaves
is darker but sometimes
lighter, yellow green
and at other times,
depending upon light,
yellow green blending
into emerald.
In contrast, tiger lily
leaves stick straight
out like a cat's tongue
stretching toward a treat,
a green with deeper growl
no purr, just bur befitting
an orange tiger.
Does anyone need to
know this?

Continuance

Portfolio of Painterly Poems

SOPHOMORE SONNET
Albion College, 1963

Fall air and flowering field yet August,
Sun rays racing through the ocher tone hay,
Silken threads of milkweed to journey must,
While southwest breezes blow across the bay.
Dainty Queen Anne's lace like a slip's border lay
Upon the field where black berries grow ripe.
To harvest them this chosen perfect day.
Leaving upon my hands crimson stains bright,
Pink, red, scarlet, then black as coming night.
Winter's blizzard shall have berry-black preserve,
But golden berry fields give us insight
From despair to spiritual reserve.
Field, cloud-filled sky, and trees above,
Revealing of God's freely given love.

Continuance

LOVE SONG

"Paint what you know."
I do, except for the English
heather that grows in the
topsoil of imagination.
Lavender, rust, purple
and golden hues, too,
against mottled, gray sky
and sometimes blue.
Painterly passion penetrates
in permanent, complementary
colors, true. My Albion,
anima you, infinite longing,
I do.

Portfolio of Painterly Poems

OLD MAN

Old Man:
I call you that-
not as a disrespectful
name for Father, since
in a detached moment of
reflection, you are an
old man with grumbles groans
but also spirit strength
of old age.
So gripe. Let it get stronger,
clearer, still. You do not
protest war or racism,
poverty or pollution; yet you notice
the pussy willows are gone.

Continuance

SUMMER

Summer is a miracle of being warm.
Summer is freedom from wool sweaters,
tights under slacks, the walls of a house.
Summer is riding bikes and picnics with friends.
Summer is watching Ernie's garden grow
toward clouds.
Summer is making love without blankets.
Summer is a miracle of being warm.

Portfolio of Painterly Poems

PROMISE

The Holy Spirit is in all
Around, within, above,
Most full within the human heart
In attitudes of love.
God calls us to the table
To find communion there
To seek Christ's presence and to share
A covenanted life.
O Lord of business, science, art,
Of parenthood and home,
 Help us to know our calling
And serve you in this world.

(A new hymn to the tune of "Our God, Our Help In Ages Past')

Continuance

DRAINED

My husband comes home,
angry,
intense,
concerned.
His tension fills me
like approaching night
absorbing the colors of
a fall afternoon.
The night comes.
Color, vitality
leave me.
I fear the dark
and chill.
And then a star appears.
I know morning will come again.

Portfolio of Painterly Poems

CHURCH MOUSE

A little church mouse
I wanted to be,
eat church supper
crumbs and feast
on Communion fare,
dwell among the hymn
books and old Bibles,
approach God cautiously
and unseen, sensing
a refuge
from all cat claws--
feline and human.
Then one day, when
making coffee,
(for the church goal-setting group)
I heard a snap and
crunch.

Continuance

My foot was caught
in a mousetrap.
Indignantly I said,
"I'm not a mouse!"
Later I thought,
"It must be better
to be human,
open,
seen,
counted,
and giving;
than to be a mouse
hiding in the wall,
never speaking
and
ever fearing
hidden traps."

Portfolio of Painterly Poems

GOOD DAY

The sun felt warm
and the wind softly
blew, rearranging my
hair like a gentle
mother's hand brushing
wispy hairs from her
daughter's face.

My child played around
me; her feet bare
and free, discovering
the grass and flat stones,
playing with older children
and finding play good.

We sipped iced tea -- my
Friend, Nancy, and I while our
children pranced and the
dog snapped at bees --
silly dog.

We talked and shared
as women do who perceive
their bond of struggle
and joy in understanding their
husbands' work.

Continuance

Winter seemed far away
with its chill and
harsh, rigid days.

I looked across the field.
The warm breeze rhythmically
rippled the grass, which
smelled clean, new.

We said, "Good bye."
Ernie, Amy and I
went home; strengthened
by grace for other days.

Portfolio of Painterly Poems

THE FIRE

The alarm rang.
Two a.m.
Another sounded
across the river,
shaking the stillness.
My husband minus
socks went downstairs
and sat in the office;
his mind calculating,
his computer brain
at work thinking,
"Westminster's alarm
rang - shortly
after our alarm.
This means a serious
fire. I don't hear
sirens on Main Street
or trucks rumbling on
Bellows Falls Road.
The fire is near by."
His analysis shifted to
compassion.
His look said, I may be long."
Our child awoke and sensing
the seriousness asked for

Continuance

her books and milk.
He returned.
His face was somber
like portraits of
Abraham Lincoln.
Life, two old sisters,
gone.
A smoking shed fire
was the cause.
The relatives and neighbors
would have to live with loss,
charred beams, sadness
and smoke in the wind.
I remembered other fires
starting in sheds
attached to old, New England
homes.
I thought about our barn.
I knew he did not blame
it on God's will; nor
give cheap comfort.
Perhaps there was embrace - a presence in
the confusion. Soon would
be the time to cry and
after that the time to get up again.

Portfolio of Painterly Poems

DEACONESS

She does as she has always done.
She is as she has always been:
loyal and there to help with
Women's Fellowship
or listen to a friend in need
or prepare Communion bread.
Her days are ordered by the tolling
of the village church bells.
Sunday mornings come.
She is in church to praise
God and find sustenance
in hymns, Scripture, thought.
The Good, as ontologically pure
as it gets, is drawn to her.
Townspeople stop to chat.
Birds flock to her feeders.
With out-stretched hands
like St. Francis of Assisi
she scatters sunflower seeds to
chickadees and jays.
The birds return her gifts with
sounds and colors which delight.

Continuance

During New Hampshire's endless mud season
she takes a car trip southward
with her husband to spot different birds.
Then in their travels together and
seeing anew, her spirit
soars like eagle's wings.

Portfolio of Painterly Poems

CHURCH TALK

They don't like this.
They don't like that.
They're very upset.
They're going to blow.

And so
I ask,
"Who are *they*?"

"Oh, I can't tell you,
It wouldn't be right.
If I told,
they would get uptight."

But it's not him,
nor her or their son.
Perhaps it's not
the whole church.
Could be *you're* the only one.

Continuance

LOVE SONNET

Destined to help each other throughout life,
The year after college we were married.
Perhaps there was a blessing in the strife.
Drawn together we did not tarry.
The best present was a silver cake knife
Engraved with wondrous words,
Through Thick and Thin.
Different drummers played and different fifes.
We journeyed onward, upward and within.
Sermons on graph paper were a big hint
That Ernie's greatest gift is engineering.
Ten years as a pastor's wife was a stint.
Inside me words were stewing and searing.
Now the rose of Sharon of my naming
Is beauty, the angled pitch of bearing.

Portfolio of Painterly Poems

MOMENTS
(September 1, 1976)

Amy and her friend Kristine
Played with the Fisher Price
doll house.
They climbed on the nursery
school's bars and hung out of
the tree house.
An older woman called
about her memorial service.
She needed assurance that
the blue and red carnations
would be given to a nursing home
patient. I listened and pensively
wrote down her message,
The girls and I picked Concord
grapes, which grow by the garage.
While picking, I thought:
"How lush and opulent and rich they
are. I feel like a queen of the harvest.
Does the purple of our Communion
juice suggest our Lord's royal reign?"

Continuance

The water in the community
pool was cooler.
Pumpkins were displayed on
Bloomfield Avenue.
This day…
Children played.
Grapes and pumpkins
matured in their seasons.
A woman looked toward her death.
I reflected in the midst of
A housewife's day and
made grape juice. My family
enjoyed a picnic supper.
Momentary glimpses of many beings
were wreathed into one day,
September first and plaited
into God,
"In who we live and move
and have our being."

Portfolio of Painterly Poems

LIGHT HAPPENS IN HAIKU

In black glass water
reflecting emerald green
our boat breaks silence.

Yellow sun rays in
pewter gray sky, November's
still, stark signature.

Purple shadows glow
on morning snow: pink light at
night—no gray in sight.

February snow:
Bluest shadows of winter
hint of spring's pastels.

Light infuses fog
with morning's golden brown and
evening's rosy peach.

Charming cat in soft
moonlight turned into a frog
in late afternoon.

Continuance

PERMANENCE

"Better on Plato
than on Schleiermacher,"
the priest-professor wrote
on my final exam.
In the ongoing tradition
of Universalist ancestors,
my mind moved "onward
and upward." Perhaps I
put more stock than I
thought in permanence,
reflected, however
dimly and discouragingly
in "death and taxes,"
and more clearly and courageously
in granite and Plymouth Rock,
signals and symbols of
human hopes and yearnings for
permeating presence and
eternal essence.

Portfolio of Painterly Poems

SHADES

Digging into the bowl of sunglasses, I found the 1980s ones with pink and green splotchy frames, sure to win the Dork of the Past award. Yet, these shades open to a better view. The blue lenses turn the sky deeper cobalt and sage a happier green. Rust and orange are more intense, without a hint of purple that you might expect with blue overlay on a sunny day. Shades of color matter, even more so shades of gray.

Continuance

FRAGMENT

In 1971, I think, the Women's Fellowship
of the First Congregational Church of
Walpole, New Hampshire went across the
river to Westminster, Vermont, to have
dinner together at a little restaurant.
That is not a surprise.
The October night was dark and crisp.
That is not a surprise.
While not the extraordinary in
the ordinary nor the superlative in the
simple, there was community.
That is not a surprise either.
At the time, I thought that the
gathering should be part of a poem
or a story, but did not know how
to artfully use this life giving fragment.
Over thirty years later, I still wonder.
That is a surprise.

Portfolio of Painterly Poems

ECLIPSE AND LIGHT

I missed the eclipse of the moon.
Yet I have seen eclipses
northeast of Boston,
southwestern shadows begun.
Without the aid of a telescope
I have spotted for some
the eclipse of welcome,
concrete barriers in minds
that block thought,
religious zeal that denies
plurality of graced experiences.
Shadows break inclusive circles.
Eclipse happens.
Before and after the lunar eclipse,
there were other sightings.
Two nights before total darkness,
the full moon lighted a circle
of white clouds framed by
a rose gold bracelet.

Continuance

The morning after shadows
passed, the morning moon shone
silver-white in a pale, blue sky.
The end or promise, implicit
in the genesis of creation, is
original loveliness. Love in a
line moves circular and straight,
spiraling towards fullness.
When the goodness of beauty is
fully intrinsic, truth is in sight.
Light happens.

Portfolio of Painterly Poems

REVELATION

Crayola retired raw umber.
Purple mountain's majesty
is in stock.
Children bear down hard
creating color memories
in muscles and minds.
Poseidon's morning mist
and sunset's rosy glow
seep in by osmosis.
Seasons change then
relinquish their colors
retained in collective
collages of consciousness.
As pigments pile,
color overflows into
rivers of rich impasto,
which empty into harbors
of the soul, held safe
in God's receiving.

Continuance

When midnight ink
covers colors that enliven
inner rooms, scratch-board
is the medium of hope.
Scrapping uncovers deeper
layers, happier hues, even
raw umber's ambiguity twixt
brown and greenish gold.
Recognizing complexity in
the whole spectrum is
revelation from an
old, stubby, peeled, worn
almost forgotten crayon.

Portfolio of Painterly Poems

TWO TRIPS

In 1954 after a family trip
to Florida, I returned to
fourth grade makeup work,
done with a pen dipped into
the inkwell on my desk.
Writing was tedious.
Content collapsed. Words,
trapped between brain and
hand, were not yet mine
to use.
I say to my inner nine-year-
old self. "Be of good cheer.
There will be inventions that
you cannot imagine. Life will
improve. Your time will come."
Fifty years later, my husband,
Ernest, and I enjoyed Florida
sun and fun. I came home to
my computer and an invitation
to submit a long manuscript.
Words flow.
Nostalgia is not for me.
Now is better.

Continuance

Portfolio of Painterly Poems

AGING

My general observation
As far back as college
Is that life can be
Held together
By the holy trinity
Of faith, Elmer's Glue
And spandex.
Now, some of us
Add to the stash
Of pillars and pills
For the sake of
Our backs, alas, alas,
A weekly dose of
FOSAMAX!

Continuance

PRIORITY

Impressions to paint,
Let the ironing wait.
Pies to bake,
Let the ironing wait.
Poems to create,
Let the ironing wait.
Walks through pastures
and pines to take,
Let the ironing wait.
My husband says, "Let's
break our routine
and eat at *Chilis."*
I need something to wear
on our merry, married
date. *Munchies* and more.
The ironing can't wait.

Portfolio of Painterly Poems

SHOPPING LIST

When shopping feels like an
Over-worn chore, I think that
Someday we will remember
When we could go to *Shoprite*
And before that *Cape Ann Market*
And before that many mega-markets
In New Jersey that were open
All night and before that a
Village *IGA* and the *Super-Duper*
Across the Connecticut River in
Bellows Falls, Vermont, and just
Before that stylish, suburban
Stores sprawling west of Boston.
Way before that I watched young,
Married women shop and thought
How romantic; in retrospect how
Silly, yet maybe Not.

Continuance

Portfolio of Painterly Poems

CORNFLOWER HAIKU

Chicory flowers
turn deeper blue after rain.
Fall sky in July.

Albino petals
on a lone chicory stem
stand out against blue.

Chicory, daisies
and Queen Anne's lace are common
yet summer's crown jewels.

Continuance

THE OTHER CHURCH

In spring 2004, I heard the phrase,
the other church across the street.
I remembered the first time I saw
the church next to the Congregational
parsonage, that was our home, as
the other church across the street.
Almost thirty years ago, nearly
three-year-old Amy on her tricycle
and I wearing my pink suede sandals
crossed the street and saw our church
from a new perspective on the other side.
In front of the Catholic Church and
the colonial home of devout Episcopalians,
I thought, "Our white church on the
village green is massive and imposing.
If I went to the Catholic Church or the
little, brown Episcopal Church, that is
modestly set back from the common, I might
not like looking at First Congregational—
the church next door and furthermore
the other church across the street."

Portfolio of Painterly Poems

MEANWHILE

In the 17th century, Pilgrims sought simplicity in a covenanted stance of purity, mindful of Word in beatitude, "The pure in heart shall see God." Meanwhile in France, Jesuits wrote books on the history and theory of dance in a playful stance, signing and stretching with arabesque to touch the heart of Love Divine. Transcendence of purity overriding the material and beauty rising above words diverge yet in the twists of history may in time turn, converge, even emerge in mutual regard. Meanwhile, there is strife and life in tension and reconciliation both begun anew among traditions sung to different tunes.

This poem was inspired by the book,
FOUR CULTURES OF THE WEST
by John W. O'Malley -- Harvard University Press, 2004

Continuance

MOVE TO MERIDEN

My husband lost his job
in Massachusetts but
landed a better one in
Connecticut the next day.
We moved to Meriden
despite warnings that
there is tarnish on the
Silver City.
Yet, Meriden is for me
a place to emerge from
behind hometown barriers
of diminishment and
shine in time poetically.
Hope gently hovers
like soft mist on the
hanging hills.
Gratitude is greatest
happiness. So be it.

Portfolio of Painterly Poems

STYLES

Evangelicals are born again.
Anglicans tell stories.
Members of the UCC make
 deliberate decisions to God's
glory. Methodists aglow warm
the world with song and with
their Baptist neighbors issue
decrees on right and wrong.
Unitarians honor many paths
while Jesuits and others
ponder foundational stepping
stones on catholic ways to prayer
and praise.
Many styles of singing raise
voices to transcendent love,
affirming treasured, turning points
to God, to Life, to Being.
Then in pondering prayerfully,
discernment may come with vision
beyond staid, tribal, partial seeing
to listening to other leanings,
multiple measures of meanings,
varied reasons for sacred seasons.

Continuance

Some religious divisions matter
not. Tolerance and trust are
sometimes taught yet often caught
when doves of peace with sterling
wings descend into hearts again
and again and again.

Portfolio of Painterly Poems

HAIKU SEASONING

Fall

Seagulls claim the beach,
one red leaf dancing on sand,
children back to school.

Purple, wild asters
in a field where horses graze,
Fall's dainty delight.

Hummingbird, purple
posies, squirrel with nut are
parts of one picture.

This fall the mallards
have three grown-up daughter ducks.
Finally success.

White butterfly on
dark green leaf, warming itself
before colors change.

Continuance

Winter

Midnight navy sky,
tan, white, doubled-pawed tomcat
curled on a child's pillow.

Two leaves blowing like
skaters on a crystal pond,
Winter's cold is here.

Bright December snow,
simplified landscape of winter,
decayed leaves vanish.

Black panther-like cat
licks the white snow. Marmalade tom
please flee to me now.

Canadian geese
swim in white reflection of
snow. Winter glory.

Yellow house, peach sky,
purple-blue clouds in sunset,
glow in winter dusk.

White streaks on window
panes—free form rectangles—they
should be in MOMA.

Portfolio of Painterly Poems

Brown, velvet ribbon
in white satin, the brook still
flowing in winter.

Large birds' nest under
cedars—birds, also lose homes
to wild, winter winds.

The birds have eaten
all the red berries: nature's
gracing tree of life.

Continuance

Spring

Late March, the sun starts
to warm New England air and
I return to spring.

Melting city snow
covers the purple crocus:
A new, strange garden.

Young red cardinal
complements peridot buds.
Essence of springtime.

Three robins check out
old nest, father, mother, last
Spring's grown baby bird.

Some father robins
help out. Others do not pitch in.
Example or genes?

Yellow bumble bee
kissing matching forsythia,
how sweet the springtime.

Portfolio of Painterly Poems

Bright yellow finch
in flowering apple tree:
Warmth of lacy spring.

Tiny red ants hold
a cake-tasting convention
in yellow kitchen.

New maple leaves fresh
sprung from buds, happy yellow
green in rain was sun.

Summer

Young girl with sand pail
bumps into wild, pink rose bush.
Petals in bucket.

Seagulls glide and dip.
Dragonflies catch soft beach breeze.
Jewels in summer sun.

Moonlight summer night:
Black and white cat weaving in
and out of shadows.

Continuance

Alert mother duck
guards two sleeping daughter ducks
on emerald grass.

Five brown sparrows sip
waterfall where koi frolic:
Pool party for birds.

Nervous, song sparrows
eating crumbs dropped by children
on concrete poolside.

Indigo bunting,
could you leave your field straw to
live in our cedars?

White flowers blooming,
perfume in the air, softly
blow summer's sweet kiss.

Portfolio of Painterly Poems

NEW ENGLAND FALL

Brown seeps into
August's emerald.
Scattering of lemon-yellow
sours summer days.
Maple leaves edged
in crimson prophesy.
As foliage and days turn
like pages in a book
of seasons, red splashes
its pure, unmixed,
paintbox hues.
Scarlet and cadmium
compete.
Brown and Emily Dickinson
win.
Red rusts then crumbles
to let sunbeams
dance on deep yellow.
Lit from above
the world is golden
until the day
of winter-white
blank canvas.

Continuance

Portfolio of Painterly Poems

SILENT WAITING

Milkweed fluff is on the ground.
Wintertime will come around.
Snow will muffle highway sounds.
Still and silent winter nights will
call forth hope for peace.
Out of silence inklings creep.
Hope fans out from thoughts
held deep, that rise it seems up
to the sky and descend aglow
on angels' wings, gently covering
all the earth with warmth and wonder,
yes, well-working, wondrous wonder
that to goodwill gives birth.

Continuance

WINTER STORM

December northeaster
undermines wharf and
wager of hope for safe
harbors.
Wave upon wave,
charcoal upon gray,
cold upon chill
penetrates couches,
coverlets, coves
of shelter,
protective images
of inner seascapes.
Fireplace flames,
Advent candles,
Day-spring in the dark
soften crusted souls
on ice and hold.
Slushy blasts pass.
Power returns.
Anxiety is not
measured by degrees.
Sun pops and peeks.
Light infusing
mystical mist
lifts eyes towards
white-gold sky.

Portfolio of Painterly Poems

WINTER RETREAT

March picks up the marching beat
Towards spring, as if the wind
Wants winter kept at bay,
All ice and cold blown away.
Yet winter stays, desire for May
Delayed in personal interiors,
Of those who savor, even favor
Cool air, clutter control, northern
Landscapes simplified by snow
When each glance through the
Window is a winter retreat into
Serenity.

Continuance

NEW HAMPSHIRE GLORY

April rain pelts the ice
on Dublin Lake.
Great puffs of fog ascend
heavenward on wings
of gusty wind.
Winter chill changes into
Spring's softer, whiter mist,
nature's transfiguration.

Portfolio of Painterly Poems

APRIL BLESSING

Robin in the snow,
I wonder if you know
the joy you bring
when you sing of spring.
Pecking through the
crusty ice, you evoke
in me fresh zest for life.
When nature and grace
converge…
Beauty is the Word.

Continuance

GIFTS OF TIME AND MINDS

Thank you, Mr. Red Robot,
on this green day in May,
for making crop circles
in my carpet while I read
poetry by thirteenth century
Buddhist Nun Abutso.*
I am not sure who my favorite
people are this moment –
librarians or electronics engineers?

 *THOUSAND YEARS OF WOMEN'S POETRY:
The voices that would not be stilled
An Anthology edited by Fiona Pagett

Portfolio of Painterly Poems

CELEBRATION IS…

Celebration springs from joy or sadness, from being with others or being alone.

Celebration is friends at a birthday party with cake and candles. Christmas is celebration.

Celebration is walking in the woods, finding moss and bark and red spotted salamanders. Lent is celebration by thinking, feeling and praying about all we have done wrong and forgotten to do right.

Celebration is blue, orange and red balloons. Easter is singing of life and love.

Celebration is shouting and dancing and blowing horns. Pentecost is celebrating the birthday of the church.

Celebration is the excitement of waiting –waiting to be old enough to walk downtown alone or waiting for summer vacation or the arrival of a new brother or sister. Advent is the celebration of waiting for Jesus' birthday.

Celebration is life: being born, growing and dying. Celebration is trusting in God.

Continuance

CLOUDY BEACH DAY

Hazy horizon gently
defines blue-gray sky
touching purple-gray
brine.
Then fog fades even
shades of graphite.
Embracing breezes boost
the salt of the sea.
Soft mist gives seaweed
deeper hue. Overcast
matches my inner view.

Fog and fleecy
sweatshirts comfort
those of somber soul
wrapped in love
not seared by sun,
society's idol of
ceaseless demand
for smiley faces
drawn upon sand.

Portfolio of Painterly Poems

BLACK ROCKS

Black Rocks, two boulders off Front Beach,
Are in ankle-deep water when the tide is low.
When the tide is high, covered five feet deep.

Children walk or swim towards them,
Sit or stand, circle round, jump or dive,
Snorkeling on days with time to spend.

Generations after generations reflect on the rocks
After beach days or sitting, thinking with dangling
Feet with joy that cannot be with money bought.

Black Rocks are eternal, permanent as they can be
The ocean ebbs, flows and moves continuously.
Black Rocks immersed in fluid tides suggest
Harmony.

Between unchanging, long-standing traditions
And new ways of perceiving, living, and caring,
Seeking balance is a thoughtful mission.

New England frugality is like a rock,
Time-honored traditions of save and swap.
The world changes like the flowing tides
Around the rocks where children dive.

Continuance

OTHER COLORS, OTHER ROCKS

I value Rockport colors and Rockport rocks yet
The year our daughter, Amy, was eleven,
Westward bound -- other rocks we sought.

The Painted Desert with hard packed sand
Was alive with flowing colors, rust, gray,
Ivory, purple-pink and tan.

Entering the desert was contemplation akin
To worship in a plain church or monastery
Where deepest silence penetrates and enters in.

The Grand Canyon quieted us -- speechless.
Miles of brown, gold, vermilion cliffs,
Layer upon layer, aged cracks of stress.

Wildlife, their habitats to mend and tend,
A friendly red squirrel and a shy black
Kaibab squirrel, stars of notes we send.

Our family was a tiny part of the picture.
Beauty settled in and ripened with joy.
We had on earth a taste of heaven
The year that Amy was eleven.

Portfolio of Painterly Poems

DAY OF THE STARFISH

One Spring day Amy's mother said,
"Let's take a walk to the beach."
So…Amy and her mother put on
their old jeans and their new sneakers.
They watered the plants,
fed the parakeet,
and scooted out the door.
On their way to the beach they saw
red and yellow tulips,
half of a robin's egg and a
family of happy robins singing in a tree,
violets coming up in the grass,
a lacy, pink tree.
They saw a man giving an
old rowboat a new coat of paint.
A sign said New Moon Beach.
Seagulls glided on the ocean breezes.
A puppy ran across the beach.
Amy and her mother walked through the dry
sand to the moist sand at the edge of the water.
They found periwinkles,
a sand dollar,
green seaweed,
brown seaweed,
a piece of smooth blue glass.

Continuance

Amy picked up a purple-red starfish
and held it in her hand. "Starfish
feel bumpy and rubbery," she said.
Amy and her mother looked together.
The little starfish gently curled
his star tips.. Amy said, "Starfish
look like a birthday party pinwheel."
"Do starfish live in the sand?" asked Amy.
"Starfish live in ocean water,"
replied Amy's mother.
Amy gently tossed the starfish back into the sea.
"Today is a day to celebrate,"
said Amy's mother.
Amy smiled and took her mother's hand.
They walked to a little store and
bought pocket bread and three tomatoes.
Together they walked home past the
rowboat with a fresh coat of paint,
the lacy tree,
and the tulip garden.
Amy and her mother shook the
sand out their sneakers.
They made egg salad sandwiches,
and spread a checkered tablecloth
on the grass.

Portfolio of Painterly Poems

They said a little prayer
thanking God for fun and food and
all the creatures of the sea.
Mother and Amy, Amy and Mother had a picnic
to celebrate the day of the starfish.

Continuance

MAINE HAIKU

Pothole is birdbath
for splashing robin
surprised by interruption.

Wild, gray eternal sea
has trendy undercurrents
of jade and green.

Turning sixty on
Friday the 13th turns out
to be graced, good luck.

Portfolio of Painterly Poems

CONNECTICUT DAYS

Two great blue herons
stop, stretch, and stalk in silence
like my heartbeat,
slowing as I, Sharon, search
and strive in solitude,
with sustained surprise that
we are here in a little condo,
overlooking a tiny pond,
where ducks and geese
accept my offerings
of daily bread.

Continuance

DAD

My father, Alberts S. Parsons, Sr.
was a postal transportation clerk
on the mail trains and one of the
first three commissioned mail
men in the town of Rockport.
He sorted mail and meanings.
He saved three messages in his
postman's inner first class slot:
1. The fatherhood of God and the
brotherhood of man.
2. Do not eat fish more than
five miles inland.
3. Two wrongs don't make a right.
I record for the RECORD-JOURNAL
his paternal insight.

Portfolio of Painterly Poems

TO SAPPHO

Scholars debate your
syntax and sexuality.
I, neither a philologist
nor philosopher, say
Thank you for your poem,
Mother and Daughter.
I am glad your mother
wore a purple headband
when she was young.
Perhaps she bought it from
ancestors of the biblical
Lydia.
Girls with golden hair
wreathed with fresh flowers
remind me that those women
from the ancient world are
not so different from
mothers and daughters,
of my day.
And did you ever find a
brightly colored headband
from Sardis for daughter,
Cleis?

Continuance

BROWN AND WHITE DOG IN OILS

I do not remember the name of the painting.
That is just as well.
I do not remember the name of the artist.
That is just as well.
I do remember the portrait of the brown
and white dog that hung on the gallery
wall outside the Rockport Art Association
kitchen where artist Joseph Jeswald
taught Saturday morning art classes
for children.
My Father came to pick me up and
looked intently at the painting.
He said, "I do not know much about
art but that dog is too perfect to be
real." Mr. Jeswald was impressed.
I, a sixth grade artist, sketched a
memory with line of thinking.
Dad drew his thoughts from perspective.
When I remember that too perfect is
not real, many things are just as well.

Portfolio of Painterly Poems

STANCE OF CHOICE

Is screaming at God
or silent submission
the stance of choice?
If relationship with God
is a creative project,
a life long love,
with the Holy Spirit
as Artistic Director,
then form follows function
as surely as yearnings
yield to lament and
contrition is enfolded
in waves of warmth
winding upward within.

Restoring relationships,
life made whole and hallowed,
is the function.

Continuance

Form must be amoeboid.
Covenant built on repression
of grief and complaint is not
sacred bond with fellow
beings or with God.
Protest must carry the pain.
Yet sometimes, "I am sorry"
are the only words worth
uttering while standing in
dark mysteries of suffering
and sin with inner eyes open
to receive the "morning star
that rises in your hearts."

Portfolio of Painterly Poems

SKY MEMORIES

The sky convinces my eyes
and me, the I, that life
is more than meets it,
oh eye and I, myself.

Sky memories, stir, sire, signal
hope that beauty touching me is
Eternal Beauty, God in three.

Purple rain clouds cleansed the
Painted Desert air and orange,
rust, yellow sand. Colors
deepened with cooling damp.

On back roads in Pennsylvania
farmlands, a blue black
night, bright with fireflies'
delight, gifted joy.

In western New York state

Continuance

fields aglow with rosy
light drank wine clouds
cupped with blessing.
Sunset promise, packaged
in mottled cobalt, lapis,
aquamarine, sapphire, infused
spirit. Turquoise rays, back-lit
by golden gleam, streamed from
streaked sky as if from the
throne of God.
Blue beamed from heaven to earth
and "all that dwell therein."

Knowing sin and sorrow, I
fell silent at the feet of
Glory.

Portfolio of Painterly Poems

DAWN

Stars sparkle
with diamond light
against changing
shades of summer night;
sapphire,
navy,
deepest midnight black,
charcoal,
granite gray,
ivory white of
daybreak rays.
Promise beckons,
upward, on.
Bright morning star
divines dusty dawn
illuminating earth,
a new beginning
pure as virgin birth.

Continuance

CONFESSIONS

God said: I AM
WHO I AM."
Jesus said: FEAR
NOT, IT IS I."
Paul said: "By
The grace of God
I am what I am."
Glory be.
I am me,
being desiring
Being.
Praising God
in Three.

Portfolio of Painterly Poems

YOU KNOW

You know, God,
It is wearing kind
Of thin. This falling
Through the cracks.
Please get back to
Me. Amen.

Continuance

RE: 9/11

Nine months of silence,
another serious ring forms
around my somber core.
Thoughts form.
Word is born again.
September shadows are
the darkest of the year.
Following 9/11, words
within break forth.
A familiar hymn rises
through accumulated
debris in memory.
"The darkness deepens.
Lord, with me abide."

Portfolio of Painterly Poems

REFRESH

Virgin birth,
Second Adam,
Participation in
"Being itself,
Beyond Being,"
New Creation:
Life spent
Without precedent.

Continuance

GARDEN VARIETY

Icicle pansies and bittersweet,
mixed images in a minor key
of promise and pain, assurance
and sprinkles of sadness,
bloom together in the Fall.
Despite winter chill, autumn
plantings of pansies will
flower again in Spring.
Orange bittersweet berries
in sunny-yellow hulls, are
reminders that life is bitter
as well as honeyed. The challenge
is meeting messy mixture with
surging trust like mighty, ocean
swells with Julian of Norwich that
"All manner of things shall be well."

Portfolio of Painterly Poems

A GRACE

Praise be
Thank Thee,
For good food
And good friends.
Good friends and
Good food make
Life taste better.
Praise be.

Continuance

CITRUS SIMMERING

Squeezing the juice of the day,
rich in joy and antioxidants for
the mind, I watched the setting
sun, large as a ruby grapefruit,
saturated orange as a tangerine,
sharing pumpkin light in gifted,
glorious glow on the icy pond.
Rippling reflections danced
against the white, ceramic banks,
reminding me of Wallace Steven's
pink carnations in winter's bowl.*
Two days before leaving for
Florida, I saw oranges.

The Poems of Our Climate

Portfolio of Painterly Poems

AUBADE

Morning light filters through
drawn draperies, the color and
texture of pared parsnips.
Harvey, our orange and white,
butterscotch sundae cat, pokes
his nose through the opening
and looks out the window.
Is there a good poem here?
No, not really. Dawned on me.
Not every scrap needs to be saved,
nor every fragment fashioned into
art. Some observations are to
simply enjoy. Like cats.

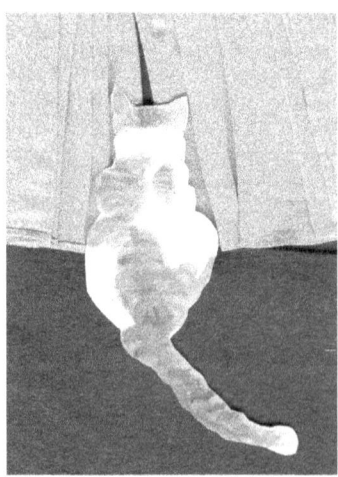

Continuance

FALL SONNET

Red apples, yellow fields, a blue horse
On a distant hill facing Ipswich Bay,
Primary colors, images not lost,
Echoing through decades of dearest days.
New England, not the only apple land,
We picked with New Jersey church
      youth groups, too.
Prime pleasures, crisp air, desires, dreams
      planned,
Yet, content with pies in sponge-wear blue.
Continuity with apple picking
Past and hope for all future children's joy,
Merge memory and present quickening,
Cherishing life, added strength of alloy.
To stop and seek, pause again then ponder,
Embracing earth, stretching yonder, yonder.

Portfolio of Painterly Poems

MOMENTUM SONNET

Ideas that drive a good life gain traction,
Car mats under tires stuck in wet snow.
Fireplace warms, thoughts sift into maxims,
Heads and pine boughs in lead crystal bow low.
Widening wonder, amazement and joy,
Silent snowfall covers clutter, visual
Noise, and quiets minds to play with word toys.
Thoughts refine ore. Gold is residual.
Heat treatment changes one's inner structure.
Experiences mesh, meld and distill
Wine in wineskins resistant to puncture,
Like life lived well, treasured, examined, milled.
Truth, Beauty and Light are revelatory
Creating pulsating colors. Grace be.

COMPLETION

Completion

PARADOX

Writing a poem is
Sharing and saving.
By grace, resisting
Temptation to horde
Spring's pastels, summer's
Greening, fall's glory,
My paint box is empty.
Yet I am filled and refreshed
By colors at rest; blending
Giving and keeping.
Colors appreciate in memory
By inner deepening,
After given away through
Poetry and paradoxically
Saved in files inside mind
Folders. Colors, like God, are
"To know and enjoy forever."

Portfolio of Painterly Poems

HAIKU HOMING

Three ducks in a row,
I thought that phrase was just an
expression. Not so.

Old black cat watching
a silent, white milkweed fluff
floating with the breeze.

Sick gull envy not
those gliding. You feel water
against broken wing.

Old man with white hair
and old dog with rusty fur
stroll in fall sunshine.

Completion

Ferry, crossing, leaves
its wake for but a moment.
Then the sand settles.

My friend, dragonfly,
died on our front steps today.
Everything passes.

Rose of Sharon blooms:
August flower of my name,
summer fullness comes.

Portfolio of Painterly Poems

TRIP HOME

The browning of August green
with fog fashioned the ride home
to Connecticut from Maine through
four New England states into a
study in shades of sage with the pop
of golden-yellow Black-Eyed Susan
in the foreground. Girl Scout color
memories, green uniforms with
yellow ties, opened gates, C. 1958

Completion

GREEN SCENE

Green changes as
seasons cycle round.
Seedtime turns into
summer.
Summer is harvest
bound.
Peridot, emerald, jade
engage hope, happiness,
deepening of summer
dreams and shade.

Portfolio of Painterly Poems

HAIKU WREATH

Small white butterfly
flits from sad, blue violets
to bright, bold tulips.
(Walpole, New Hampshire, 1973)

Small white butterfly
in New Jersey garden too,
city manse haiku.
(Verona, New Jersey, 1976)

Small white butterfly
kisses my cheek in blessing
after graveside rite.
(Rockport, Massachusetts, 1980)

Completion

Small white butterfly
lands on lavender asters,
full circle haiku.
(Meriden, Connecticut, 2005)

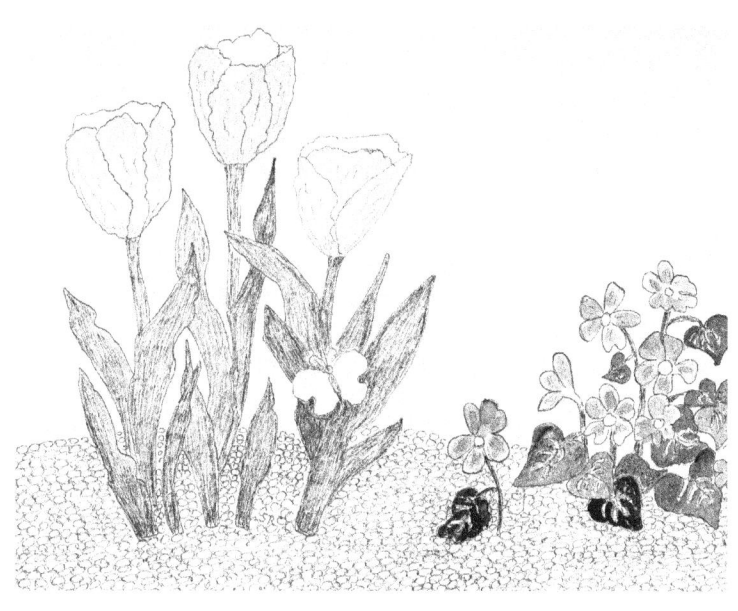

Portfolio of Painterly Poems

ON ROUTE
(To Westmoreland, NH)

When *Brook Street* becomes
River Road, the stream flows
Into the Connecticut River
Winding to the sea.
Driving along the rolling road,
Curvy like life with spice,
All impulses, ambitions, drives
To glide along life's ongoing
Currents flow, crest then overflow
The banks of imagination and
Spread into a high-water mark
Of peaceful momentum towards
Telos, the present telescoping
Into purpose, goal, fulfillment,
End, destiny, infinity and the
Universal ocean of humanity.

Completion

SONNET FOR DORIS

It takes a big subject for a sonnet.
Love, death, life, Walpole's late, true friend, Doris.
Kind words, church life, on Christ her mind was set.
Glory to God in bird song was her bliss.
Boston University, B.R.E.
Church jobs were scare, so young children she taught,
In a one-room school to read, write and see,
Find their life in joy, sought, not sold nor bought.
Trusting, she put herself in God's huge hands.
Age ninety-eight she lived to be fully
Alive before angels sang with their band
To call her home to peace and Ralph, goodly.
Nature writing, woven-pink thread, throughout,
She bids us grow - add to our love account.

Portfolio of Painterly Poems

ETERNAL AUBADE

After the settling of the night
when barely remembered,
agitated dreams dissipate,
there comes a dawning of
the light. Mental processes
illuminate. All that is good
rises through invitation.
Past pain is almost forgotten
and harmful people forgiven
in the promise of a new day.
Not quite perfect, nor complete,
notably yet rarely for those
whose lives are put on hold
by need for revenge or ripped
apart by ravishing realities,
this earthly pattern is, or so
it seems to me to be, reflection
of entrance to eternity.

Completion

There is hope, even perception,
from imagining refracted
beams: inner stars restoring,
maturing, perfecting, shining
prisms bright.
Enter diamond light.
After the *valley of the shadow*
ancestral angels holding lanterns
line the path to the door opening
to *joy in the morning*.

Portfolio of Painterly Poems

WIDENING STREAM

"Look at those rosy peaches,
How soft and fuzzy to the touch,
One for you and one for me,"
Said shepherd-farmer Frank to
His wife Anna, who in her
Prime taught Sunday School
At the church called *Riverside*.

Completion

As life streamed toward the
Transcendent river, gratitude
Flowed into enthusiasm for
Each other, singular stones,
Every flower and all sheep.
The forest became a cathedral
With blue spruce buttresses,
Cedar incense and a pine needle
Carpet old and deep as the
Membership records of Pilgrim
Seekers with faith leaps.

Winter's drifts piled three feet
High. Stained glass, sunset sky,
Back lit, black, leaden branches
Infusing beauty into the landscape
Of pure, hoar-crystal snow that
Holds the Puritan soul in tow.
The kitchen window glowed
With yellow light like a tiny,
Votive candle in the night.

Portfolio of Painterly Poems

IMAGINING

It is hard to picture Liberty,
Missouri, without Bill and Alvira,
second parents to my husband
since his college days, worshipping
in the Second Baptist Church
every Sunday. Their earthly praise
has passed.
Yet, I can imagine infinite song.
I cannot easily envision a white,
clapboard cottage in Pigeon Cove,
Massachusetts without my high
school friend, Beverly's mother,
named Bessie like my grandmother,
opening heart, home and hearth
to foster children.
Yet, I can imagine a time
when others will serve.

Completion

I cannot foresee a world where
all people find nurture and pass
on caring as do those who know
freedom and build safe harbors.
Yet, I can imagine possibilities.
I cannot see, except imaginatively,
Jesus' promise of his Father's
house of many mansions.
Yet, someday I will **not** imagine.

Portfolio of Painterly Poems

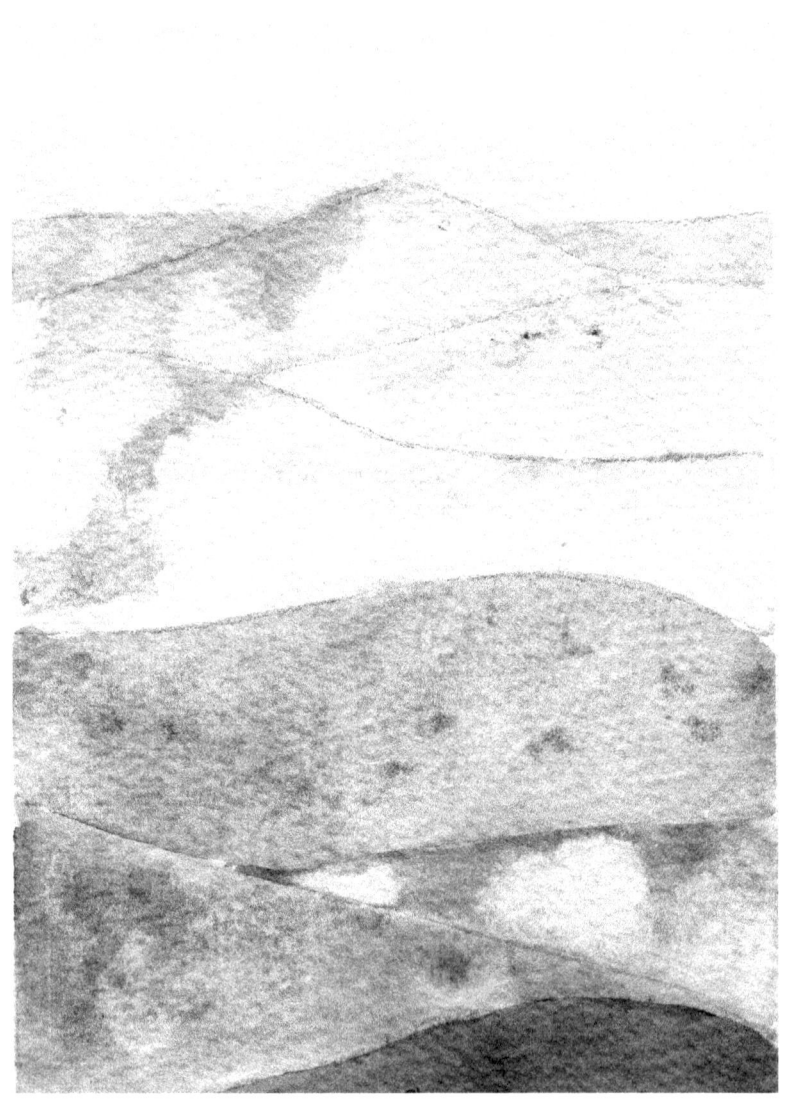

Completion

GETTING THERE

Once in a while, on automatic
Pilot, I say, "Don't think you
Can get there from here."
Nonsense, of course, with
Enough time and travel
Fare, one can get to just
About anywhere.
Yet, some places are harder
To reach than are others,
World peace with sisters
And brothers or that vista
Of beauty, "To be happy at
Home" that Samuel Johnson
Understood as the ultimate,
End of ambition, often
Derailed on the journey.
So I comb my collection
Of old New England sayings
And conclude that for most
Of us travelers, "It's going
To take some figuring."

Portfolio of Painterly Poems

THE MIND OF GOD

Is the mind of God
like a computer
where files are never
lost?

And every desire,
single joys,
each unhappiness
can be called up
one at a time;
embraced and weighed
in a just and loving
presence.

Completion

Or does God
work in collage
seeing juxtapositions,
unexpected connections,
intersection of conflicting
yearnings?

And in chaos, Wisdom
pictures holy order
by eliminating all
that destroys
peace in community
while pasting together
the pieces, which
evoke power to bless.

Portfolio of Painterly Poems

ONE PURE NOTE

A young man with long hair in shadowed light
Walked into the woods on the path by the pond
Reflecting Lamentation Mountain, a mound of might.

He gracefully carried a recorder flute
Or perhaps it was an ancestral Indian pipe
And blew a perfect note, so clean, so pure, not moot.

The purest note, in this world, I have ever heard
Like Adam before his toddler's tumble from Eden's womb
Like Lamentations' blue-bodied man before evil surged.*

If purity by nature must turn gray, decay
Then maintenance of divine spark is holy work
Ensure devotion. Dullness is derivative of delay.

Invitation of all things lovely and filled with light
Refresh; renew the self, the mourning soul
And shelter with many kinds of mounds of might.

Completion

Growing up and old is what people do
To love, to work, to search for meaning
To give back to life one pure, clear note
Is to bask in God and in beauty soak.

* Lamentations 4:7

Portfolio of Painterly Poems

Completion

TRANSLATION

The social worker called,
"It is time to consider
hospice care for your
husband's mom."
Directed by an existential
imperative to translate
biology into theology,
I made a mental note,
a *post it* in my mind
to memorize by rote.
"The skin is breaking down"
means, *"Dissolving into God."*

Portfolio of Painterly Poems

BLUE SONNET

Blue morning glories reach from ground to sky,
Jacob's ladder connecting earth, heaven.
Singing, angel muse patiently stands by.
Pure hue, glory, loveliness is leaven.
Hagar looking upon the face of God
Lived. So shall those whose gaze is strong enough
To embrace the icon nourished in sod.
Beauty so deep sadness is joyful hush.
Fathers of Israel saw beneath God's feet
A sapphire pavement. Hallow, praise, chant.
Sing in Heaven's City evil's defeat.
Foundations of treasured, precious blue stone,
Power, purest presence, God's face alone.

Completion

POSTSCRIPT

If I have another book of poetry,
it will be called **FOOTNOTES**,
be my notices in verse afterthoughts
or short, shining, silver, strivings
of strength; endnotes, to be more
precise, written at the close of life.
Footnotes can be addendum adding
publishing costs, annoying details
or, if annotated, a delightful tracing
of intellectual development.
Perfectly placed commas, colons and
parentheses are woven into the fabric
of statements documenting thought
in the mold. Tiny, tidy summaries
polish the author's prose gold as
writing poetry buffs rough intimations
and shines experience into words,
even footnotes.

Acknowledgements

Thank you to the RECORD-JOURNAL of Meriden, Connecticut that has published most of the poems.

The prose poem, *Celebration Is,* was published in the former journal *Colloquy,* issue of December 1970.

The poem/story, *Day of the Starfish,* was published in POCKETS, issue of June 1995. Thank you to POCKETS/THE UPPER ROOM for returning the copyright to me.

The poem, *The Mind of God,* was published in *The Unitarian Universalist Christian* issue of Spring/Summer 1993 Vol. 48, Nos.1-2. Thank you to The Unitarian Universalist Christian for returning the copyright to me.

www.ingramcontent.com/pod-product-compliance
Lightning Source LLC
Chambersburg PA
CBHW072149160426
43197CB00012B/2308